A dental timeline

c. 3000 BC

Earliest-known evidence of tooth treatment, from ancient Egypt.

c. 500–1600

Tooth-pullers and barber-surgeons remove rotten teeth; doctors make painkillers, tooth polishes and mouthwash.

c. 500 BC

Greek doctors treat gum disease and crooked teeth.

1728

The word 'dentist' is first used, by brilliant French expert Pierre Fauchard.

c. 2700 BC

Chinese doctors use acupuncture (treatment with needles) to ease tooth pain.

c. 1600–1750

New tooth experts call themselves 'operators for the teeth'.

c. AD 100

Romans use herbal mixtures and magic to treat toothache. Tough army doctors pull out teeth.

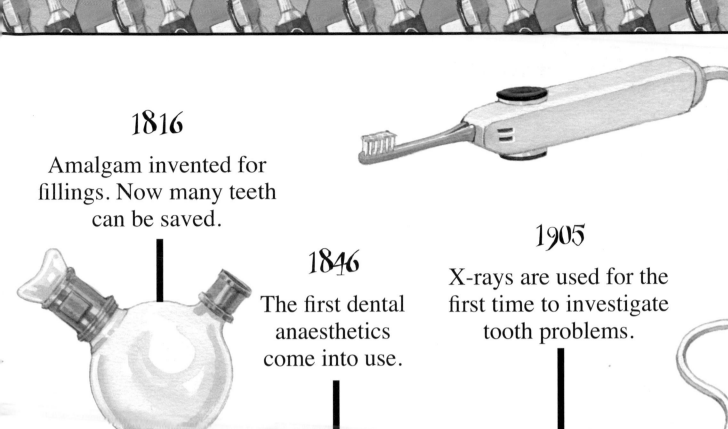

1816

Amalgam invented for fillings. Now many teeth can be saved.

1846

The first dental anaesthetics come into use.

1905

X-rays are used for the first time to investigate tooth problems.

1840

First training college for dentists opens, in Baltimore, USA.

1980–present

Technology brings new treatments. Cosmetic dentistry becomes popular.

1700–1850

False teeth are made from animal teeth, bone and ivory – and teeth from dead humans are re-used.

1850–1950

Tooth troubles increase as people eat more sugar.

Tips for top teeth

Want to keep your smile looking lovely? Then care for your teeth this way:

Brush your teeth – up and down, side to side – for at least two minutes twice a day. A dentist or dental hygienist will show you the best way to do this.

Wait half an hour after eating or drinking before brushing your teeth. Brushing too soon rubs acid made by mouth bacteria into your teeth.

Eat tooth-friendly foods. Milk, cheese, fish, grains, fruit and vegetables will all help you stay healthy and help your teeth grow strong.

Always brush your teeth before you go to bed.

Don't eat too much sugar, or have many sweet or fizzy drinks.

Use dental floss or little interdental brushes to clean the gaps between your teeth and between teeth and gums.

You can rinse your mouth out with mouthwash – but not straight after you've brushed your teeth, or you'll wash the toothpaste away.

Use fluoride toothpaste and a clean toothbrush (hand-powered or electric). Don't rinse with water afterwards. Any traces of toothpaste left on your teeth will go on killing cavity-causing bacteria.

Last but not least, see a dentist for regular check-ups. Ask your dentist about fluoride coatings to help your teeth stay strong.

Author:

Fiona Macdonald studied history at Cambridge University and at the University of East Anglia. She has taught in adult education and in schools and universities, and is the author of numerous books for children on historical topics.

Artist:

David Antram was born in Brighton, England, in 1958. He studied at Eastbourne College of Art and then worked in advertising for 15 years before becoming a full-time artist. He has illustrated many children's non-fiction books.

Series creator:

David Salariya was born in Dundee, Scotland. He has illustrated a wide range of books and has created and designed many new series for publishers in the UK and overseas. David established The Salariya Book Company in 1989. He lives in Brighton with his wife, illustrator Shirley Willis, and their son, Jonathan.

Editor: **Stephen Haynes**

Editorial Assistant: **Mark Williams**

PAPER FROM
SUSTAINABLE
FORESTS

Published in Great Britain in MMXV by
Book House, an imprint of
The Salariya Book Company Ltd
25 Marlborough Place, Brighton BN1 1UB
www.salariya.com

ISBN: 978-1-910184-62-2

© The Salariya Book Company Ltd MMXV

3 5 7 9 8 6 4

A CIP catalogue record for this book is available from the British Library.
Printed and bound in Malaysia.
Reprinted in MMXIX.

Visit
www.salariya.com
for our online catalogue and
free fun stuff.

You Wouldn't Want to Live Without™

Dentists!

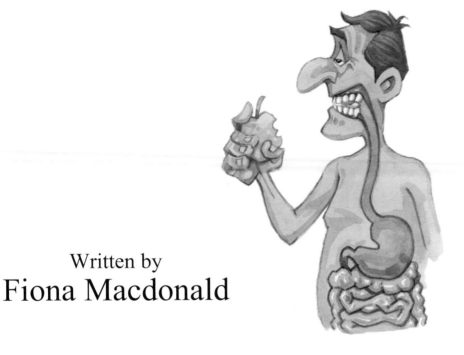

Written by
Fiona Macdonald

Illustrated by
David Antram

Created and designed by
David Salariya

BOOK HOUSE
a SALARIYA imprint

Contents

Introduction

Did you know? There was a time, not long ago, when there weren't any dentists. When people got terrible toothache and their teeth turned black, got loose, rotted, and fell out. It was disgusting – and you can read all about it in this book! But today, we don't have to suffer through toothaches or worry about having a gappy smile. Why? Because we have expert dentists to help us. Dentists use amazing technology to repair and replace damaged teeth. They relax us with music and friendly smiles. They cure our pain, and are caring and gentle. Just as important, they teach us how to care for our teeth so they stay healthy and look good. If we're smart, we go to the dentist every six months to get our teeth checked out. We really wouldn't want to live without dentists!

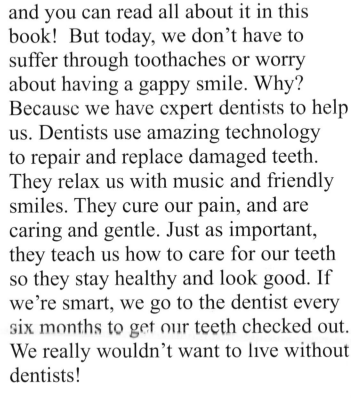

Go on – smile!

Terrific teeth

Yes, we've all got teeth, but why? What are teeth for? First, and most important, we need teeth for eating. They are the world's first, and best, food processors. Like machinery in our mouths, teeth chop and grind, crunch and crush, chomp, chew and gnaw all the food we eat. They then mix the food with saliva (spit), so it slides down easily into our stomachs. Without teeth, we'd find it difficult to eat – and hard to stay alive.

We also need teeth for talking. They help our lips and tongues make all kinds of different sounds. Just look at yourself in a mirror, say a few words, and watch those teeth move!

HOW MANY teeth do you have? It depends how old you are. Babies are born without teeth, then 20 milk (first) teeth push through their gums. These fall out when children reach 6 to 12 years old, and 32 adult teeth grow in their place, ready to last a lifetime!

ADULT HUMAN TEETH grow in four different shapes and sizes:

8 incisors: flat, with sharp edges for cutting and nibbling.

4 canines: fang-shaped and pointed, for stabbing and gripping.

8 premolars: with rounded points, good for chewing and crunching.

8 molars: big and flat, used for grinding.

4 third molars or 'wisdom teeth': a spare set of molars, right at the back of the mouth, that appear much later than the rest of the teeth.

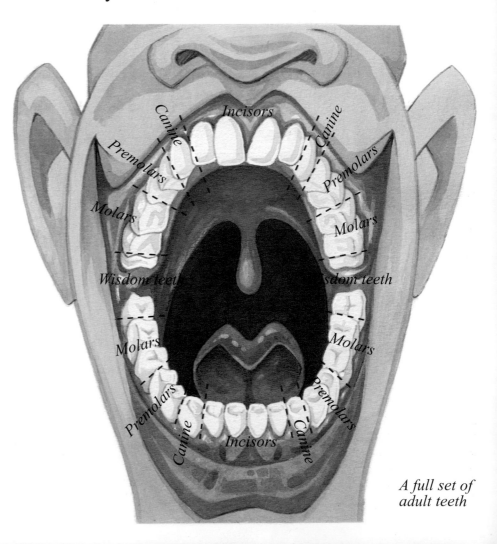

A full set of adult teeth

CHEWING GETS our digestive system going. When our teeth crush food, saliva starts to break it down so our bodies can use the nourishment it contains. Our stomachs and intestines digest the food still more. Then our blood carrics nourishment from the digested food to every part of our body, and we stay strong and healthy.

Saliva

Stomach

Intestines

Tooth types

Different animals have different types of teeth, to help them process the different foods they need to survive:

NIBBLING. Rats and mice have huge **incisor** teeth, great for gnawing and nibbling. Their incisors keep on growing all the time as the hard food wears them away.

TEARING. Lions, tigers and other cats have sharp, curved **carnassial** teeth that cut flesh like knives or scissors.

Roar!

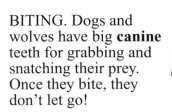

Nibble

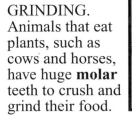

Snarl

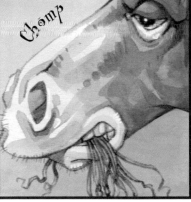

Chomp

BITING. Dogs and wolves have big **canine** teeth for grabbing and snatching their prey. Once they bite, they don't let go!

GRINDING. Animals that eat plants, such as cows and horses, have huge **molar** teeth to crush and grind their food.

Toothless = helpless?

We all need our teeth, to eat and talk and smile. But what happens when they get damaged, or we lose them? In the past, there was no easy way to repair or replace teeth chipped in accidents, knocked out in battle or ground down by chewing tough, gritty food. Disease, poor nourishment and old age made teeth wobble, crack and crumble, and many teeth rotted simply because they were not kept clean. Life long ago with teeth troubles would be painful, difficult and probably smelly. You'd be toothless – and helpless.

A healthy adult tooth

Enamel

Dentin

Pulp

Gum

Root

Nerves and blood vessels

Cementum

Enamel protects the inside of the tooth.

Dentin produces chemicals that strengthen the enamel.

Pulp contains nerves and blood vessels.

Cementum holds the roots in place in the jaw.

Past tooth troubles

HORRIBLE HOLES. Cavities (holes) let bacteria spread deep inside teeth to infect pulp, nerves and jaws.

YUCKY INFECTIONS Bacteria living around teeth made people feel ill – and made their breath smell revolting.

HEART TROUBLE. Blood carried bacteria from rotten teeth to the heart, which stopped it working properly.

GHASTLY GRIN. Black, broken teeth and a gappy smile were not a good look for anyone, even a long time ago.

DAMAGE AND DECAY. Teeth are tough, but they can still be damaged in many different ways.

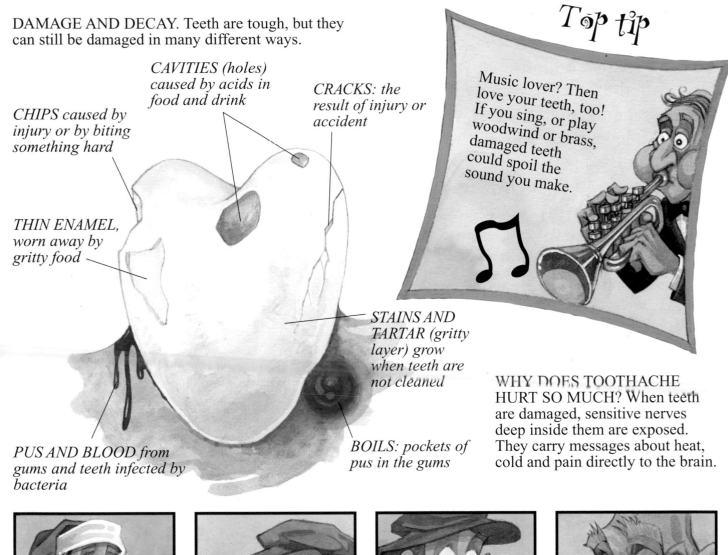

CAVITIES (holes) caused by acids in food and drink

CRACKS: the result of injury or accident

CHIPS caused by injury or by biting something hard

THIN ENAMEL, worn away by gritty food

STAINS AND TARTAR (gritty layer) grow when teeth are not cleaned

PUS AND BLOOD from gums and teeth infected by bacteria

BOILS: pockets of pus in the gums

Top tip

Music lover? Then love your teeth, too! If you sing, or play woodwind or brass, damaged teeth could spoil the sound you make.

WHY DOES TOOTHACHE HURT SO MUCH? When teeth are damaged, sensitive nerves deep inside them are exposed. They carry messages about heat, cold and pain directly to the brain.

LOST LOOKS. Without teeth, people's faces changed shape. They had hollow cheeks and shrunken gums.

MOUTH DISEASE. Broken, dirty teeth hurt the inside of the mouth and caused nasty ulcers and boils.

FOOD FAILURE. With no teeth for chewing, people could only eat soft, slushy foods. They might starve!

SPEECHLESS. It was hard to speak clearly without teeth – and just as difficult for listeners to understand!

First find your frog

If you lived thousands of years ago and had tooth troubles, who would help you? In ancient Egypt there were doctors; in ancient Greece you could go to a temple and hope to be cured in a dream. Elsewhere, you might ask a traditional healer to ease your pain with risky remedies. North African village healers would put a dead mouse in your mouth. In Scotland, they'd tell you to suck a caterpillar. In Asia, you'd swill poisonous mouthwash to kill (imaginary) toothworms. The Aztecs of ancient Central America found biting on a hot chilli pepper surprisingly soothing.

Early tooth treatments

This won't hurt a bit.

Grind

BRRR! BRRR! Ancient Egyptians drilled holes in jawbones to let pus from rotten teeth and gums drain away. Very risky, very painful.

BUZZ OFF! To treat toothache, ancient Egyptians rubbed gums with sweet, sticky honey from bees – gentle, soothing and mildly antiseptic, but rarely a cure.

This will numb the nerve.

PINS AND NEEDLES. Chinese healers stuck needles into patients to numb pain from diseased teeth. This is called acupuncture. It may have helped, sometimes.

Top tip

Got toothache today? Please don't try old cures, or magic, or strange herbal remedies. A modern dentist will ease your pain, quickly and *safely*.

MAGIC BY MOONLIGHT. Ancient Roman writer Pliny the Elder (AD 23–79) recorded this weird and wonderful remedy. If you have an aching tooth, go to a garden at midnight when the moon is full, find a frog, pick it up, open its mouth and spit into it. Then ask the frog – politely, of course – to take your pain away.

COUGH! SPLUTTER! To ease tooth troubles, ancient Greeks breathed poisonous smoke from burning leaves. We don't know how many died from the poison.

SIZZLE, SIZZLE! Greek doctors used red-hot wire to cut away infected gums and diseased flesh in the mouth. Absolutely terrifying!

CLUNK! CRUNCH! Roman army doctors carried big metal forceps (gripping tools) to rip out rotten teeth. Quick, but horribly painful!

Blacksmith or barber-surgeon?

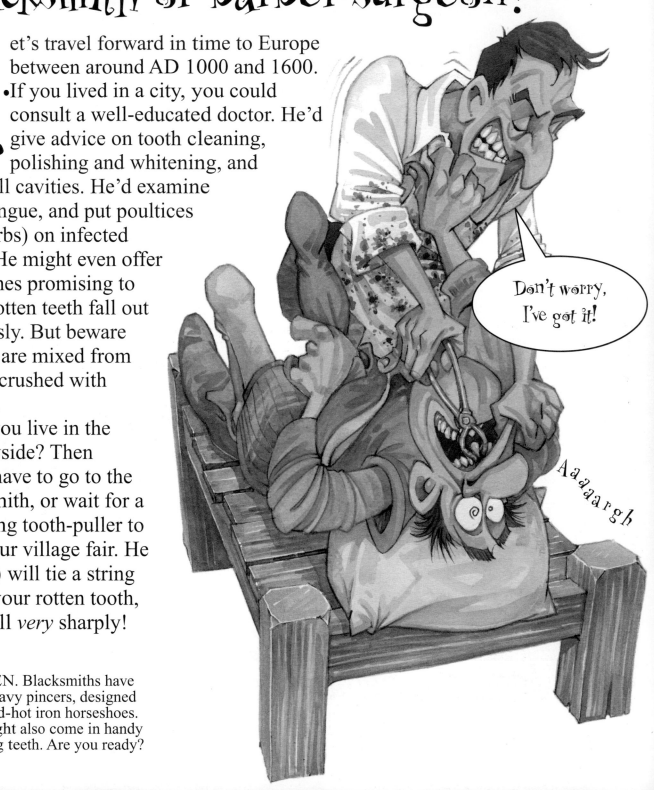

L et's travel forward in time to Europe between around AD 1000 and 1600. If you lived in a city, you could consult a well-educated doctor. He'd give advice on tooth cleaning, polishing and whitening, and try to fill cavities. He'd examine your tongue, and put poultices (hot herbs) on infected gums. He might even offer medicines promising to make rotten teeth fall out painlessly. But beware – these are mixed from lizards crushed with beetles.

Oh, you live in the countryside? Then you'll have to go to the blacksmith, or wait for a travelling tooth-puller to visit your village fair. He (or she) will tie a string round your rotten tooth, then pull *very* sharply!

Don't worry, I've got it!

Aaaaargh

IRON MEN. Blacksmiths have strong, heavy pincers, designed to hold red-hot iron horseshoes. These might also come in handy for pulling teeth. Are you ready?

FAITH HEALING. St Apollonia, a Christian leader from North Africa, was martyred (killed for her faith) in AD 249. Before she died, enemies pulled out all her teeth. For hundreds of years afterwards, Christians believed that Apollonia could cure toothache.

ON YOUR WAY TO TOWN? Then – if you're a man – pop in to see your nearest barber-surgeon. He'll cut your hair, trim your beard, shave your whiskers, set your broken bones, cut off any damaged limbs – and pull out your teeth. You might even meet a friend there. A barber's shop is a great place for gossip.

Top tip

Got to get rid of a rotten tooth, but feel terrified? Then listen to the tooth-puller's drum! Its pounding beat will drive all thoughts and feelings from your mind – and drown out your cries of pain.

What can I do for you, sir? Tooth pulled, shave, haircut?

Could you afford to ask an expert?

It's around 1750, and have you heard the latest? There's a new type of expert in town! They call themselves 'operators for the teeth' or, sometimes, 'dentists'. They still pull out rotten teeth, but they also try all kinds of new treatments to keep mouths healthy. They spend years studying science and medicine, learning about teeth and bones and blood and how our bodies work. They write books. They're very clever. No doubt you'll feel safe in their hands. But – here's the problem! – they also charge very high fees.

PELICANS

Bolster often causes injuries

Grip tooth between claw and bolster, then press other end to lever tooth out.

Claw hooks over tooth

TOOTH KEY

Twist handle like a key to lift tooth out of jaw.

Bolster

Claw

Claw tightens around tooth

New name, new knowledge

IN 1728, French scientist Pierre Fauchard published a brilliant new textbook about teeth. He called it *Le Chirurgien Dentiste* (The Dental Surgeon). This was the first time the word 'dentist' appeared. It came from the French word *dent* (tooth) and is still used in English today, together with *dental* (to do with teeth) and *dentistry* (the science of tooth treatment).

TO PULL OUT TEETH, dentists and operators use a special new implement called a tooth key, first made around 1730. They say it's much safer than the old-fashioned pelican. That's been used by doctors for over 200 years – and it often breaks patients' jawbones!

Emergency!

NEED TOOTH TREATMENT? Can't find a barber-surgeon? Can't afford a new-style dentist? Then look around town for a jeweller or a wigmaker; he (or she) will be skilled with their hands, and will use the tools of their trade to care for you. Or you could ask an apothecary – a trained maker and seller of medicines. He'll be used to helping patients.

Pliers

Wigmaker

Drill

Jeweller

Apothecary

Painkiller

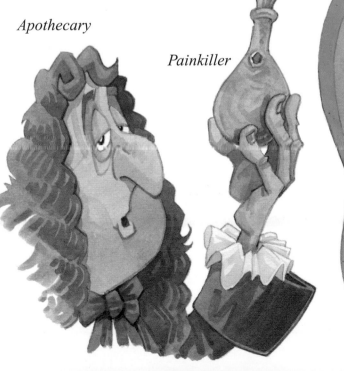

Top tip

Want to be an 18th-century dentist? You'll have to start young! Sign on as an apprentice (working trainee) when you're 11 years old. By 25, you'll know enough to set up in business on your own.

Dragons and roses

That's what you'll find in the first-ever English book about teeth. Written by Charles Allen in 1685, *The Operator for the Teeth* contains information about many tooth topics – from childhood teething troubles to luxury tooth polish made from expensive, exotic ingredients: powdered coral, dragon's blood (actually a kind of gum from tropical trees) and sweet-smelling rosewater.

Would you favour false teeth?

Well! Here's more new tooth technology! As well as offering safer tooth-pulling and scientific mouth care, new expert dentists have been fitting patients with fancy false teeth. Long ago, Egyptians, Greeks and Romans made teeth from bone or hardwood, and tied them to surviving tooth stumps with thread or gold wire. In Central America, Maya craftsmen fashioned replacement teeth from seashells. But these 18th-century teeth are carved from precious ivory, trimmed, polished, then fitted into smile-shaped frames of ivory or bone.

Or you could try experimental tooth transplants. Dentists take teeth from dogs, sheep, or even dead people, and fix them into gappy jaws. The transplants look lifelike, but patients risk catching very nasty diseases.

From hippo to Mr President: George Washington's false teeth

Tusks

GOTCHA! Hunters in Africa kill a fierce hippopotamus and cut off its tusks.

HIGH PRICE. The hunters sell the valuable tusks to Arab traders.

IT'S A DEAL! The traders sell the clean, polished tusks – now called hippo ivory – to European dealers.

WATERLOO TEETH. That's what transplanted human teeth are called, because dentists took so many teeth from dead bodies after the famous Battle of Waterloo in 1815.

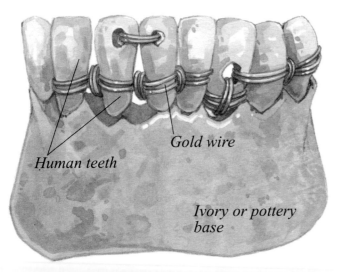

Gold wire

Human teeth

Ivory or pottery base

ACROSS THE ATLANTIC. The ivory travels by sailing ship from Africa to America.

GREENWOOD CARVES the ivory into human-looking teeth and fixes them to a curved base.

SMILE, PLEASE! US President George Washington (1732–1799) wears his new false teeth with pride.

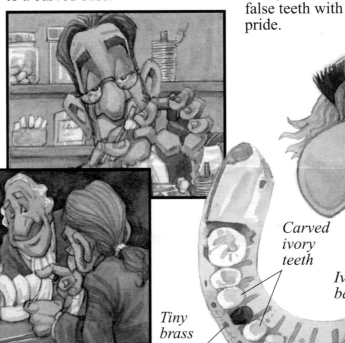

Carved ivory teeth

Ivory base

Tiny brass screws

IN THE USA, dentist and false-teeth expert John Greenwood (1760–1819) buys the ivory.

Would you brush tooth troubles away?

Elizabeth I (ruled 1558–1603)

If you wanted fresh-feeling teeth in the past, which cleaning method might you prefer? Perhaps chewing herbs? (The ancient Greeks liked fresh mint.) Maybe rubbing your teeth with powdered chalk, Roman-style, or scrubbing them with salt? You could scrape stains away with crushed eggshells, slurp a herb-and-vinegar mouthwash, or massage your teeth and gums with rags soaked in wine.

Don't trust those old treatments? Well, help is at hand! Since 1780, toothbrushes have been sold in Britain. Jars of ready-mixed toothpaste first appeared in 1873 in the United States, although toothpaste tubes were not invented until 1892.

SWEET TOOTH. Queen Elizabeth I of England ate sweet treats, hoping to sweeten her breath. Alas, the royal gnashers turned black and crumbled. Why? See pages 24–25.

Brushes from bushes

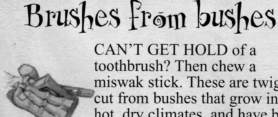

CAN'T GET HOLD of a toothbrush? Then chew a miswak stick. These are twigs cut from bushes that grow in hot, dry climates, and have been used in Asia and the Middle East for over 1,000 years. In Arabia, the Prophet Muhammad encouraged his followers to chew them, and they are still used for cleaning teeth by many Muslims today.

Chewed end of twig is a toothbrush

Hold still!

You can do it!

Today, experts say we should brush for at least two minutes, at least twice a day, and always at bedtime. For more top tips on tooth care, see the front of this book.

MOTHERS' ORDERS.
After toothpaste came into use, first in the United States and then in Europe, advertisements urged everyone to brush their teeth. The British government told mothers that if they didn't care for their children's teeth, they were failures!

Toothbrush timeline

WE DON'T KNOW when toothbrushes were invented, but Chinese people were using them soon after AD 1000. It took hundreds of years for them to reach Europe, but after that:

1780

1954

1780, UK: brushes made of cow bone and pig bristles.

1938, USA: easy-to-clean nylon toothbrush invented.

1960s, USA: first cordless toothbrush.

1885, USA: mass production of toothbrushes.

1954, Switzerland: first electric toothbrush.

1992, USA: ultrasonic toothbrush uses high-speed vibrations to remove plaque.

1938

Will fantastic fillings save your fangs?

Today we know what causes cavities (holes) in teeth, and can take action to prevent them. But, until around 1750, tooth decay was a mystery. Repairing rotten teeth was almost impossible; early fillings – stone chips, bits of cork, scraps of metal – all fell out or crumbled. But in 1816, French dentist Auguste Taveau invented amalgam (silver mixed with mercury), and it was tough enough to last a lifetime. Although slightly poisonous, amalgam fillings saved countless teeth, and prevented much pain and suffering. Now dentists could repair teeth instead of removing them!

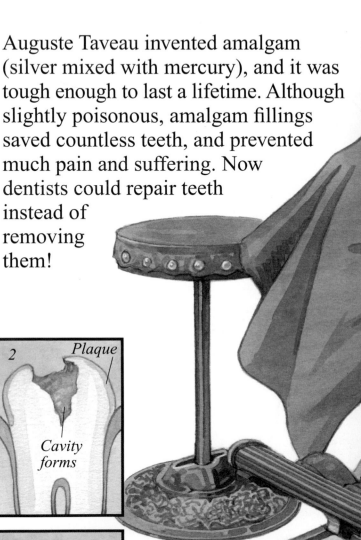

Dentist's stool

Look out: bacteria at work!

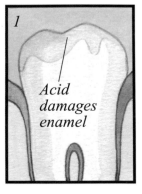

1. Around 1750, Pierre Fauchard finds that eating sugar produces acid in the mouth. The acid attacks tooth enamel and forms cavities.

Acid damages enamel

2. Around 1890, US dentist Willoughby Miller shows that this acid is made from sugar by a sticky layer of bacteria, called plaque, that grows on teeth and gums.

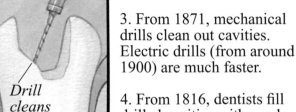

Plaque

Cavity forms

3. From 1871, mechanical drills clean out cavities. Electric drills (from around 1900) are much faster.

Drill cleans cavity

4. From 1816, dentists fill drilled cavities with amalgam. Gold (from 1820) and porcelain (from 1871) are softer but safer alternatives.

Amalgam filling

In the dentist's chair, c. 1880

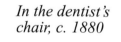

How it works

Flossing fights the need for fillings. Dental floss – fine plastic thread or tape – can reach into tiny gaps between teeth and gums to remove scraps of food and plaque that your toothbrush has left behind.

Tip of drill

Assistant turns wheel to power the drill

Rinse and spit here

Reclining chair for patient

Dare you join the new profession?

magine that you are a bright young person living around 1900. At first, you dreamed of being a doctor. But now you're wondering, 'Dare I change my plans?' Well, you would not be alone if you did. In Europe and the United States, hundreds of men and women are now training to be dentists. These well-educated new dentists are well paid and respected, and have trained assistants to help them. They work in purpose-built surgeries, using new equipment to diagnose teeth troubles and new techniques for tooth repairs. And – thank goodness! – they have new ways of making dental treatment much less painful.

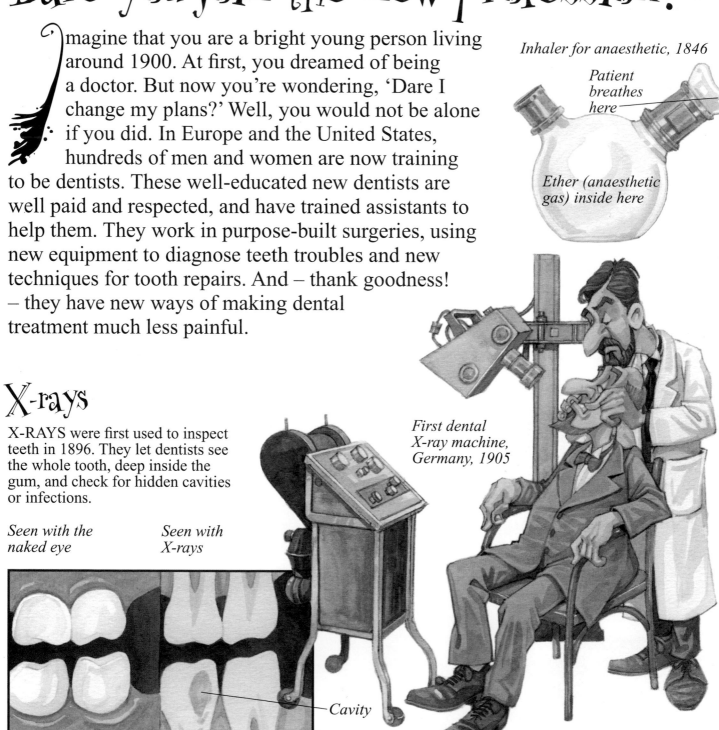

Inhaler for anaesthetic, 1846

Patient breathes here

Ether (anaesthetic gas) inside here

First dental X-ray machine, Germany, 1905

X-rays

X-RAYS were first used to inspect teeth in 1896. They let dentists see the whole tooth, deep inside the gum, and check for hidden cavities or infections.

Seen with the naked eye

Seen with X-rays

Cavity

Root of tooth

ANAESTHETIC GASES (left) made patients unconscious. They were first used by American dentists in 1846. Reclining chairs (invented 1832) made it easier for dentists to work on teeth and kept patients comfortable.

Sleeping like a baby! He won't feel a thing.

Top tip

Salute the pioneers! The first dentists' training college opened in Baltimore, USA, in 1840. The first woman to qualify as a dentist was American Lucy Hobbs, in 1866.

Needle injects anaesthetic

Nerve

LOCAL ANAESTHETICS were used by dentists from around 1880. They numbed a nerve, making the area around it pain-free. The patient stayed awake.

Anaesthetic gas

Prevention is better than cure

In spite of new technology and better-trained dentists, by the early 20th century, in Europe and the United States, many people's teeth were worse than ever. Why? Poverty and sugar! Poor families could not afford toothpaste or toothbrushes, and had no money to pay dentists. But sugar was cheap, so sweet, sticky foods became favourite treats. Schools, governments, dentists and toothpaste manufacturers all tried to tell people how to care for their teeth. By the 1950s, Americans could buy dental insurance. And in some European countries, new national health services provided free dental check-ups for all.

Bread and beans – what a feast!

BEFORE cheap sugary foods came in, you'd eat lots of bread, beans, meat, cheese and vegetables at a party.

SWEET IGNORANCE. Ordinary people did not know that mouth bacteria turned sugar in sweet foods to acids that attacked their teeth.

Owww

You can do it!

Sugar and acid in juice and fizzy drinks rot your teeth. So do your teeth – and your health and weight – a favour. Don't have more than one sweet drink per day.

THE FLUORIDE STORY. In 1901, American student dentist Frederick McKay noticed that farmhands in Colorado Springs had extra-tough teeth. He did tests, and found that local drinking water contained a natural chemical, fluoride, that makes tooth enamel stronger. Today, fluoride is added to water by many governments, and also to toothpaste and mouthwash.

AFTER cheap sugar arrived, you'd feast on cakes, biscuits, doughnuts, jam sandwiches and sweet drinks.

Go on, smile – please!

Today, thanks to dentists, our teeth may not be rotten, but they can still be crooked, gappy or sticking out. They might be broken after an accident, or stained by food and medicine. Less-than-perfect teeth can be painful and make eating difficult. We might even feel ashamed of them. But dentists can help!

Cosmetic dentistry – the art of making teeth look good – has a long history. Past peoples shaped their teeth or studded them with gold to boast of age, rank, status and bravery. Ancient Greeks straightened teeth with wires; modern dentists still fit braces to create a perfect smile. And some dentists will still decorate teeth – if you really want – with harmless glued-on diamonds.

A mouthful of metal

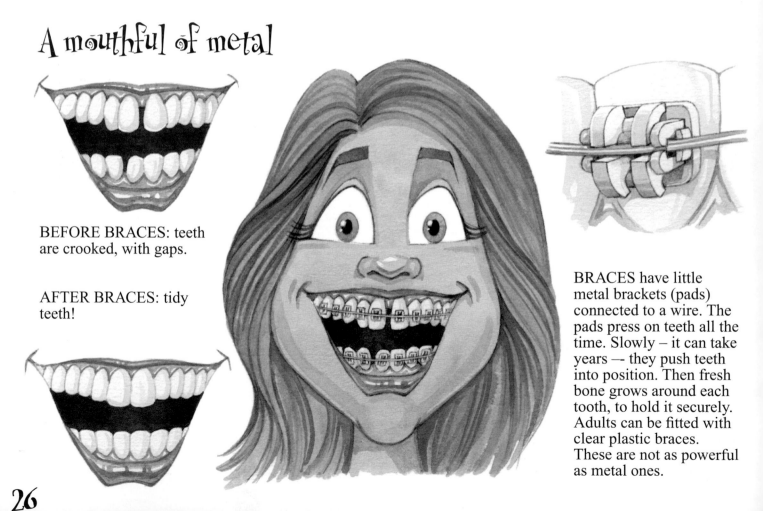

BEFORE BRACES: teeth are crooked, with gaps.

AFTER BRACES: tidy teeth!

BRACES have little metal brackets (pads) connected to a wire. The pads press on teeth all the time. Slowly – it can take years –- they push teeth into position. Then fresh bone grows around each tooth, to hold it securely. Adults can be fitted with clear plastic braces. These are not as powerful as metal ones.

Oooh, he's so handsome!

Top tip

White is not always right! Natural teeth grow in many different colours, shapes and sizes. Today, bright white teeth are fashionable, but home bleaching treatments (invented in 1989) can weaken tooth enamel. Beware!

FILM STARS and supermodels flash dazzling smiles as part of their glamorous image. Often, their 'perfect' teeth have been created by cosmetic dentistry.

YOU CAN TAKE IT WITH YOU! Old-style Russian gangsters wore false teeth made of gold, so no-one could steal their treasure.

SENSE OF BELONGING. In the past, some people in Africa and Asia filed their teeth into points to show membership of a tribe.

PROUD AND BRAVE. In Central America, top Maya warriors decorated their teeth with discs of real gold. Fitting them must have been very painful.

BLING! BLING! Money to burn? Then copy today's rock stars and adorn your teeth with real jewels.

27

The teeth of tomorrow?

Looking back over thousands of years, don't you feel fortunate? Nowadays, tooth treatments are better and safer than ever before. But one big dental problem remains: how to get tooth care for everyone, rich or poor.

Already, many of us keep our own teeth all life long. Soon, we may have genetically modified teeth that won't rot, personalised replacement teeth grown from stem cells, ozone gas treatments to kill mouth bacteria and vaccines against tooth decay. With the grim and painful past behind you, and this exciting future ahead, would you really want to live without dentists?

CAT SCANNERS take 3-D X-rays of teeth, roots, gums and jaws.

AND RELAX! A comfortable chair helps patients lie still and keep calm.

High-tech treatments

BRIDGE THAT GAP. Bridges (custom-made rows of teeth fixed to gums) and implants (stuck-in teeth) fill gaps. They are much more comfortable and hygienic than old-style false teeth.

CROWNING GLORY. Crowns are new teeth made of porcelain, toughened glass or metal. They fit over stumps of broken teeth.

LASERS (beams of high-powered light energy) burn away diseased gums.

28

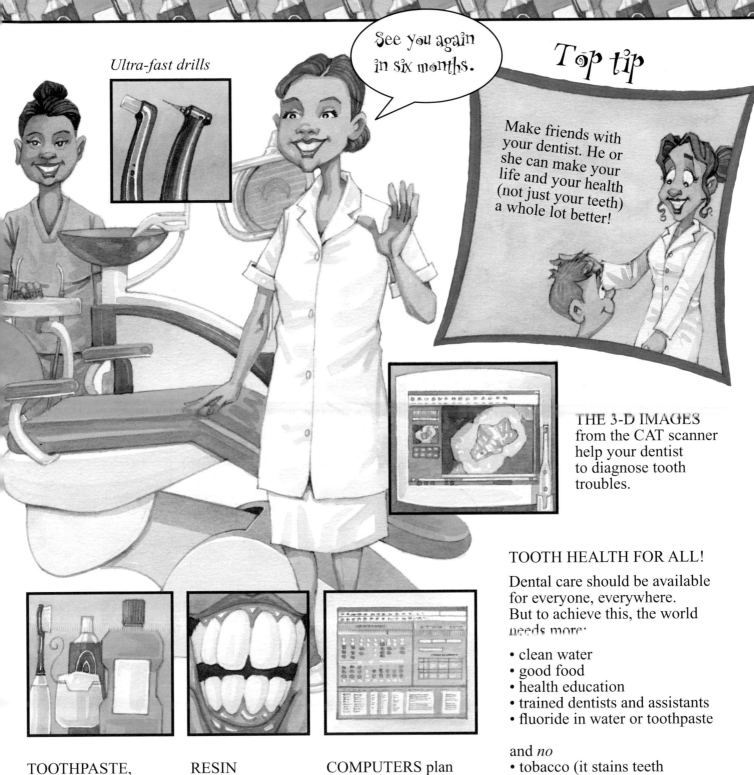

Ultra-fast drills

See you again in six months.

Make friends with your dentist. He or she can make your life and your health (not just your teeth) a whole lot better!

THE 3-D IMAGES from the CAT scanner help your dentist to diagnose tooth troubles.

TOOTH HEALTH FOR ALL!

Dental care should be available for everyone, everywhere. But to achieve this, the world needs more:

- clean water
- good food
- health education
- trained dentists and assistants
- fluoride in water or toothpaste

and *no*
- tobacco (it stains teeth and causes mouth disease).

TOOTHPASTE, toothbrush, mouthwash and floss keep teeth healthy.

RESIN COATINGS on old teeth make them look new.

COMPUTERS plan treatments, monitor patients' progress and keep records.

How can we help this happen?

Glossary

Acupuncture A traditional Chinese treatment using needles to ease pain.

Amalgam A mixture of silver and mercury used to fill teeth.

Anaesthetic A drug that stops pain.

Antiseptic Able to kill bacteria and stop infections.

Apothecary A supplier of medicines.

Bacteria Bugs or germs; some of them can cause disease.

Barber-surgeon A worker who pulled out teeth and gave simple medical care.

Blacksmith An ironworker.

Blood vessels Veins, arteries and capillaries – tubes that carry blood around the body.

Bridge A row of replacement teeth fixed to the gums.

Canines Fang-shaped, pointed teeth for stabbing and gripping.

Carnassials Curved teeth for cutting flesh, in meat-eating animals such as cats, lions and tigers.

CAT scanner A device that produces digital 3-D images of the body.

Cementum A layer of cells that fixes tooth roots to gums and jawbones.

Cosmetic dentistry Treating teeth to make them look good.

Crown A hollow replacement tooth fitted over the stump of a broken tooth.

Dentin The inner layer of a tooth. It produces chemicals to keep the tooth enamel strong.

Dentist A trained expert who cares for teeth and treats tooth troubles.

Enamel The hard, white, shiny outer layer of a tooth.

Ether A gas used as an anaesthetic.

Floss Plastic thread or ribbon for cleaning between teeth and gums.

Genetically modified With genes changed by scientists. (Genes are chemicals that tell cells in living creatures how to function.)

Hygienist A trained worker who cleans and cares for teeth.

Implants Replacement teeth fixed into gums one at a time.

Incisors Flat teeth at the front of the mouth, for nibbling.

Ivory A hard, white substance from animal tusks.

Laser A beam of high-powered, focused light energy.

Martyred Killed for religious beliefs.

Miswak A bush from which twigs are cut to make simple toothbrushes.

Molars Big, flat back teeth for grinding.

Nerves Fibres that carry signals to the brain.

Operators Early experts who studied tooth care and supplied false teeth.

Pelican A hook to pull out teeth.

Plaque A sticky layer of bacteria on teeth and gums.

Premolars Teeth with rounded points.

Pulp The soft, spongy centre of a tooth.

Resin Sticky gum that sets hard.

Rosewater Scent made from rose petals.

Saliva (spit) Liquid from glands close to the mouth; helps digest food.

Stem cells Cells that can grow into different body parts.

Surgery A dentist's workplace.

Tartar A hard, gritty layer of plaque.

Tooth key A key-shaped hook to pull out teeth.

Tusk An extra-long front tooth in some animals.

Wisdom teeth A spare set of molars at the back of the mouth.

Index

Top tooth traditions

To people in the past, teeth were mysterious and rather worrying. They were part of a living body, but fell out and did not decay. It's not surprising that many strange superstitions and traditions grew up around them:

• In medieval England, parents feared that children would have to hunt for lost baby teeth when they died. So they burned baby teeth.

• Some people still say that a gap between the front teeth is a sign of long life… or of wealth… or of a loving nature…

• Viking warriors paid good money for baby teeth because they believed these brought victory in battle.

• Hunters worldwide wore jewellery made from the teeth of bears, wolves and sharks. They hoped this would give them a share of the animals' power.

• In Europe and the United States, carrying horse teeth in your pocket was said to guard against toothache. Some people claimed that teeth from a dead human were even better.

• German children believed that a rat stole children's teeth. Unlike the Tooth Fairy, the rat didn't leave anything in return.

• Folktales from many countries tell of blood-sucking vampires with teeth like animal fangs.

• Old people are sometimes said to be 'long in the tooth'. Teeth don't really grow longer with age, but they sometimes look longer because the gums have shrunk.

Beastly teeth

- Rats' and rabbits' front (incisor) teeth never stop growing. They have to be worn away by eating, otherwise they stick into the gums above and below them.

- Sharks grow up to 50 rows of teeth, side by side.

- Dogs, cats and many other hunting animals show their teeth in a snarl, as a warning sign of attack. But chimpanzees show teeth as a sign of fear.

- Some snakes have hollow teeth that inject poison when they bite.

- Giraffes have front teeth in their bottom jaw only.

- Elephants' tusks are outsized teeth, used for digging up food and for fighting. Elephants' back teeth are also enormous: each one can measure 30 cm across and weigh more than 2.5 kg.

- Crocodiles grow new, bigger teeth all their lives – up to 3,000 of them for each animal. The old teeth drop out.

- The narwhal, a type of whale, has a single tusk sticking out of its mouth. This can grow to about 3 metres long. It is mostly used to detect prey and sense location.

- Have you ever heard the saying 'as rare as hen's teeth'? Yes, that's right: hens and other birds don't have any teeth at all!

Did you know?

- Human mouths contain almost 250,000 different types of bacteria. Regular teeth-cleaning will keep them under control.

- Tooth enamel is the hardest part of the human body. It's even stronger than bone.

- Teeth can last longer than all other human body parts – some have lasted thousands of years.

- Everyone's teeth are different, just like fingerprints. Since 1878, teeth have been used by doctors and police investigators to identify dead bodies after accidents and at crime scenes.

- Teeth start forming in our mouths long before we are born. That's one reason why it's important for pregnant women to eat healthily.

- Our teeth are bigger than we think! Two-thirds of each tooth (the root) is hidden inside the gum. We only see the other third.

- In the United States today, tooth decay is the second most widespread health problem, after the common cold.

- In China, 20 September is 'Love Your Teeth Day'. It reminds everyone to look after their teeth properly.